SEL CAREERS

THERAPIST

BY STEPHANIE FINNE

BLUE OWL BOOKS

TIPS FOR CAREGIVERS

Social and emotional learning (SEL) helps children manage emotions, create and achieve goals, maintain relationships, learn how to feel empathy, and make good decisions. The SEL approach will help children establish positive habits in communication, cooperation, and decision-making. By incorporating SEL in early reading, children will be better equipped to build confidence and foster positive peer networks.

BEFORE READING

Talk to the reader about different types of therapy.

Discuss: Therapists work in different areas of mental health and well-being. Have you ever been to therapy? If so, what kind?

AFTER READING

Talk to the reader about therapists and mental health.

Discuss: How do therapists help others? What can you talk to a therapist about? How could talking to a therapist help you or someone you know?

SEL GOAL

Some students may struggle with self-awareness. Help readers build these skills by learning to stop and think about what they are feeling. How do their emotions affect how they behave? What do they need to do to be mindful in the moment? Discuss how learning to do these things can help them.

TABLE OF CONTENTS

CHAPTER 1
What Is a Therapist? ... 4

CHAPTER 2
How Do They Help? ... 10

CHAPTER 3
Going to Therapy ... 18

GOALS AND TOOLS
Grow with Goals ... 22
Try This! ... 22
Glossary ... 23
To Learn More ... 23
Index ... 24

CHAPTER 1

WHAT IS A THERAPIST?

Julia has **anxiety**. She can't stop worrying about her family, friends, and school. She worries so much she has trouble sleeping.

To help her feel better, she meets with a therapist. Therapists help people talk about emotions. They teach patients how to **cope**. Julia's therapist helps her recognize anxious patterns in her thoughts.

CHAPTER 1　5

Therapists help people of all ages. Some work in schools. Others work in clinics, hospitals, or their own office.

Therapists can **diagnose** conditions like **depression**. They help people build skills to feel better.

TRAITS OF A THERAPIST

Therapists are patient. They are good at listening and solving problems.

6 CHAPTER 1

CHAPTER 1   7

Therapists need a four-year college degree and a **master's degree**. Some have a **doctorate degree**. Therapists get a **license** for the state in which they work.

CHAPTER 1   9

CHAPTER 2

HOW DO THEY HELP?

Therapists help people understand and talk about their emotions. Some therapists help patients show their emotions through art. Drawing or painting what they feel helps patients name their emotions.

Amari's therapist helps him practice **positive self-talk**. Amari works on turning "I can't" into "I can't *yet*."

CHAPTER 2   11

Lila talks to her therapist about a **bully** at school. They act out how she feels when she is bullied. Then, they talk about how it would feel to stand up to the bully. They also talk about who she can go to for help at school.

PLAY THERAPY

Therapy can include playing. A therapist will watch a child play alone and with others. The way a child plays can show their concerns without them saying anything.

CHAPTER 2

CHAPTER 2

Therapists also help families. Arthur's family started therapy when his dad remarried. Their therapist helps their **blended family** work together. They talk about **communication**. Therapy helps them get along better.

CHAPTER 2 15

Jenny's parents are getting divorced. Jenny now has two homes. Her dad lives in a separate apartment. Jenny meets with a therapist to talk about how she's feeling. Therapy helps her cope with changes in her **routine**.

CHAPTER 2

CHAPTER 2

CHAPTER 3

GOING TO THERAPY

What happens when a person goes to therapy? First, the therapist watches, listens, and learns about the patient. The therapist makes an **assessment**. It helps them understand the patient in order to help.

Therapists plan what type of therapy will be best for each patient. They may have meetings with parents or teachers. Why? So they can all work together. They want to find the best way to help.

CHAPTER 3   19

Therapists help us talk about emotions, face fears, and solve problems. They help us be our best selves!

WHEN DOES THERAPY END?

Therapists will meet with patients as often as needed. They help until the problem is solved. It may take a long time or just a little while.

CHAPTER 3

CHAPTER 3

GOALS AND TOOLS

GROW WITH GOALS

Therapists must be able to empathize with others. Try working on these goals.

Goal: Pick one person in the room. Think of one thing that person may be feeling. How would that feel for you?

Goal: Think of a struggle one of your friends has had. Make a list of all the emotions that struggle may bring up. Think about how the struggle would make you feel.

Goal: Therapists are good listeners. Practice for this career by listening to someone today.

TRY THIS!

One thing therapists teach is developing positive patterns of thinking. When you're not feeling confident, you might tell yourself you aren't good enough or that you can't do something. When that happens, pause. Take a deep breath. Visualize yourself succeeding. What does that look like? How do you feel?

GLOSSARY

anxiety
A feeling of worry or fear.

assessment
An evaluation of someone's abilities or needs.

blended family
A family that consists of a couple and their children from their current and all previous relationships.

bully
Someone who frightens or picks on others.

communication
The sharing of information, ideas, or feelings with another person through language, eye contact, or gestures.

cope
To deal with something effectively.

depression
A medical condition in which you feel unhappy, irritated, or hopeless, can't concentrate or sleep well, and aren't interested in activities you normally enjoy.

diagnose
To recognize a condition or disorder by signs and symptoms.

doctorate degree
A degree given by a college or university after at least four years of additional study following a master's degree.

license
A permit or permission granted by a group to do something.

master's degree
A degree given by a college or university usually after one or two years of additional study following a bachelor's degree.

positive self-talk
Words or thoughts that are helpful and make you feel good about yourself and your abilities.

routine
A practiced sequence of actions.

TO LEARN MORE

Finding more information is as easy as 1, 2, 3.

1. Go to www.factsurfer.com
2. Enter "**therapist**" into the search box.
3. Choose your book to see a list of websites.

GOALS AND TOOLS

INDEX

anxiety 4, 5

art 10

assessment 18

bully 12

clinics 6

college 9

communication 15

cope 5, 16

depression 6

diagnose 6

emotions 5, 10, 20

family 4, 15

friends 4

hospitals 6

listening 6, 18

parents 16, 19

patients 5, 10, 18, 19, 20

play 12

positive self-talk 11

problems 6, 20

school 4, 6, 12

skills 6

teachers 19

worrying 4

Blue Owl Books are published by Jump!, 5357 Penn Avenue South, Minneapolis, MN 55419, www.jumplibrary.com

Copyright © 2024 Jump! International copyright reserved in all countries. No part of this book may be reproduced in any form without written permission from the publisher.

Library of Congress Cataloging-in-Publication Data

Names: Finne, Stephanie, author.
Title: Therapist / by Stephanie Finne.
Description: Minneapolis, MN: Jump!, Inc., [2024]
Series: SEL careers | Includes index.
Audience: Ages 7–10
Identifiers: LCCN 2022062089 (print)
LCCN 2022062090 (ebook)
ISBN 9798885246439 (hardcover)
ISBN 9798885246446 (paperback)
ISBN 9798885246453 (ebook)
Subjects: LCSH: Psychotherapists–Juvenile literature. | Psychotherapy–Vocational guidance–Juvenile literature.
Classification: LCC RC480 .F552 2024 (print)
LCC RC480 (ebook)
DDC 616.89/140231–dc23/eng/20230111
LC record available at https://lccn.loc.gov/2022062089
LC ebook record available at https://lccn.loc.gov/2022062090

Editor: Eliza Leahy
Designer: Molly Ballanger
Content Consultant: Michal Rischall, Ph.D., L.P.

Photo Credits: LightField Studios/Shutterstock, cover (therapist); Pixel-Shot/Shutterstock, cover (patient), 3, 19; FatCamera/iStock, 1; Studio Romantic/Shutterstock, 4, 5; nullplus/Shutterstock, 6–7; Kdonmuang/Shutterstock, 8–9; SrdjanPav/iStock, 10; triloks/iStock, 11; KatarzynaBialasiewicz/iStock, 12–13; fstop123/iStock, 14–15; Tom Wang/Shutterstock, 16–17; ben bryant/Shutterstock, 18; FG Trade/iStock, 20–21.

Printed in the United States of America at Corporate Graphics in North Mankato, Minnesota.